science
fair

OCT -- 2002

Science Alive!

Heat

CRABTREE
Publishing Company
www.crabtreebooks.com

How to use this book

Each chapter begins with experiments, followed by the explanation of the scientific concepts used in the experiments. Each experiment is graded according to its difficulty level. A level 4 or 5 means adult assistance is advised. Difficult words are in boldface and explained in the glossary on page 32.

Crabtree Publishing
www.crabtreebooks.com

PMB 16A, 350 Fifth Avenue,
Suite 3308, New York
New York 10118

612 Welland Avenue,
St. Catharines, Ontario,
Canada L2M 5V6

**Published in 2002
by Crabtree Publishing Company**

Published with Times Editions
Copyright © 2002 by Times Media Private Limited

Series originated and designed by
TIMES EDITIONS
An imprint of Times Media Private Limited
A member of the Times Publishing Group

Coordinating Editor: Ellen Rodger
Project Editors: P. A. Finlay, Carrie Gleason
Production Coordinator: Rosie Gowsell
Series Writers: Darlene Lauw, Lim Cheng Puay
Series Editor: Oh Hwee Yen
Title Editor: Daphne Rodrigues
Series Designers: Tuck Loong, Loo Chuan Ming
Series Picture Researcher: Susan Jane Manuel

Cataloging-in-Publication Data

Lauw, Darlene.
    Heat / Darlene Lauw & Lim Cheng Puay.
      p. cm. — (Science alive)
    Includes index.
    Summary: Simple text and experiments describe and demonstrate the principles of heat and how heat energy is produced.
    ISBN 0-7787-0559-5 (RLB) — ISBN 0-7787-0605-2 (pbk.)
    1. Heat—Experiments—Juvenile literature. [1. Heat. 2. Heat—Experiments.
3. Experiments.] I. Lim, Cheng Puay. II. Title.
    QC256 .L38 2002
    536'.078—dc21

2001042422
LC

Picture Credits
Marc Crabtree: cover; Bes Stock: 7 (top), 14, 15 (right), 18, 27, 26 (top), 31 (right); Hutchison Library: 6; NASA: 22;
Science Photo Library: 10 (top), 11, 15 (left), 19 (top), 23 (left), 30, 31 (left); Travel Ink: 23 (right);
Trip Photo Library: 1, 7 (bottom), 10 (bottom), 19 (bottom), 26 (bottom)

Printed and bound in Malaysia
1 2 3 4 5 6—0S—07 06 05 04 03 02

INTRODUCTION

We see the effects of heat everyday: wet clothing drying in the sun, ice melting in a glass of water, and bread rising in the oven. We also feel heat when we walk in the sunshine or hold our hands under a dryer. Heat is a form of energy that comes from the movement of tiny **molecules** and **atoms** that make up **matter**. Learn all about heat by reading this book and doing the science experiments.

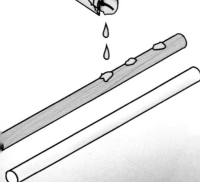

Contents

Steam power!

Different objects rely on different sources, or types, of energy. The wind is a source of energy that can move a sailboat. Motorboats use **electricity** to drive their propellers. Try this experiment to see if you can make an object move without wind, batteries, or fuel. Ask an adult to help you.

■ Ask an adult for help

Difficult — 5
        — 4
Moderate — 3
        — 2
Easy — 1

You will need:
- A raw egg
- A stiff metal wire
- A bowl
- Water
- Plasticine
- A candle stub
- An aluminum foil food tray
- A tub
- A lighter or matches

Rocket boat!

1 Gently wash the egg. Using the stiff metal wire, carefully poke a small hole through the egg from one end to the other.

WATCH OUT!
Be careful when lighting the candle. Check that the eggshell and wire frame are not too close to the flame.

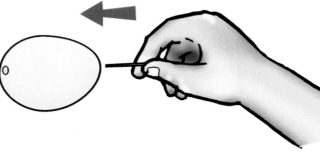

2 Hold the egg low over the bowl, and blow through one of the holes. The yolk and egg white will come out the other end and fall into the bowl.

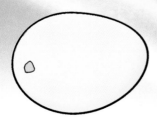

3 Clean the inside of the eggshell by running water through the holes. Let the eggshell dry. When dry, seal the hole at the wider end with a piece of plasticine.

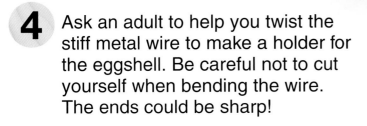

4 Ask an adult to help you twist the stiff metal wire to make a holder for the eggshell. Be careful not to cut yourself when bending the wire. The ends could be sharp!

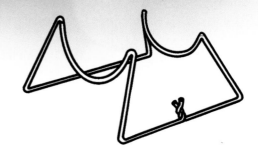

5 Place the wire frame in the food tray. Fill the eggshell with a little water, and put it on the wire frame. Place the candle under the eggshell, but do not light the candle yet. Place the tray in a bathtub filled with water.

6 Now, ask an adult to light the candle for you. After a few minutes, watch what happens. The boat will thrust forward by steam power.

Is it magic or science?

When the water in the eggshell was heated, it evaporated. This means that the water changed from a liquid to a gas. Water **vapor** formed inside the eggshell and built up pressure, until it escaped through the tiny open hole in the shell. The force of the escaping water vapor pushed the boat forward. This is called steam power.

Heat energy in everyday life

Before **diesel** power was invented, trains powered by steam engines carried travelers over long distances. A steam engine works like the eggshell in the experiment. A steam train has a boiler, which is a tank filled with water. Pipes run through the water in the tank. These pipes carry hot air from a coal or wood fire. The air in the pipes heats the water in the tank, and produces steam. The steam enters the steam engine and pushes **pistons**. The pistons produce a force that turns the wheels of the train.

An old-fashioned steam train

A steam outlet at a geothermal power plant. At geothermal power plants, wells are drilled deep into the Earth, where temperatures can reach 356°F (180°C) or higher. This heat source from the Earth can be used as energy. The first geothermal plant was built in 1904 in Larderello, Italy. There are now geothermal plants throughout the world.

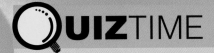

QUIZTIME

Can steam engines be used for other purposes?

Answer: Yes. Steam engines can be used to generate electricity. Such engines are called steam **turbines**. The steam generated rotates turbines. These turbines operate generators, which in turn produce electricity.

Heat energy in nature

Geysers are naturally occurring hot jets of water and steam that shoot out from the ground like fountains. They provide a natural source of energy. Hot rocks deep in the Earth heat underground water to boiling point. The hot water rises and enters cracks in the ground. Cooler water from rocks near the ground level also enters these cracks. When the two waters meet, the hot water heats the cooler water. Steam forms and squirts out of the cracks. The water and steam burst out of the ground into the air. This is called a geyser eruption.

These gauges measure the steam pressure in the boiler of a steam-powered train.

Did you know?
In 1803, an Englishman named Richard Trevithick built and tested the first steam train. Twenty-three years later, American engineer John Stevens designed and tested the first American-built steam train.

DANGEROUS STEAM!

Steam and boiling water have the same temperature: 212°F (100°C). Steam holds more heat energy than boiling water does. This is why steam causes more painful scalding than boiling water! Since steam holds so much heat energy, it is very important to keep the pressure in steam engines at the correct level. If the pressure of the steam rises too high, an explosion can occur!

Sun power!

The sun is the source of all life on Earth. Every second, it gives off 386 billion billion megawatts of energy! That is enough energy to meet the Earth's electrical power needs for centuries! Try this activity to see what solar energy, or energy from the sun, can do.

Difficult — 5
— 4
Moderate — 3
— 2
Easy — 1

You will need:
- An outdoor tap
- A pail
- A thermometer
- Pen and paper
- A dark-colored hose with a plug

Make your own solar heater!

1 On a sunny day, run some water from the outdoor tap into the pail. Place the thermometer in the water for one minute. Write down the temperature, then pour out the water.

2 Attach one end of the hose to the tap. Seal the other end with the plug. Coil the hose, and leave it on the ground under direct sunlight.

3 Fill the hose with water. Then turn off the tap.

4 After about an hour, remove the plug. Release the water into the pail. Using the thermometer, carefully take the temperature of the water. Compare it with the first result. What has happened? The water in the hose has been heated by the sunlight!

Energy from the sun can be converted into electricity by a device called a **solar cell**. Solar cells work best on bright sunny days, when the sun's rays are strong. Look what happens when we focus the sun's rays to generate electricity from the solar cell.

More power!

1 Buy the solar cell and the **galvanometer** at an electronics store, or ask your teacher if you can borrow them from school. Any galvanometer that measures a direct (one-way) electrical current in the range of 0 to 10 milliamps can be used.

■ **Ask an adult for help**

Difficult — 5
4
Moderate — 3
2
Easy — 1

You will need:
- A solar cell
- A galvanometer
- Plasticine
- A cardboard box (for example, a shoebox)
- Two pieces of insulated wire
- A magnifying glass

2 Using the plasticine, stick the back of the solar cell to the side of the cardboard box, so that the box supports the cell.

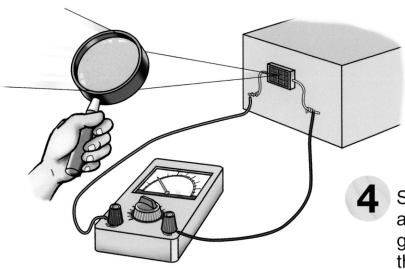

3 Ask an adult to help you connect the solar cell and the galvanometer using two pieces of insulated wire.

4 Shield the solar cell from light, and note the reading on the galvanometer. Then expose the cell to light, and watch the needle move slightly.

5 Now, position the magnifying glass to focus a small but bright patch of light onto the cell. Watch the galvanometer needle swing farther than before. This shows that more energy, or a stronger **current**, is flowing. The magnifying glass collects more energy from the sun than can be captured by the cell alone!

Where does the sun's energy go?

Most of the sun's energy flows out into space. Only a tiny amount reaches the Earth. Less than two percent of the solar energy we receive is changed into wind and wave energy or used by plants to make food. This means a lot of energy from the sun is wasted!

Solar panels on the roof of a house are tilted in a direction that allows them to catch as much sunlight as possible.

Solar-powered

Solar power is very useful. We use solar power for some of our energy needs. Solar panels on the roofs of some houses are used to heat water. This water is pumped through pipes on the back of the panels. Sunlight on the panels warms the water in the pipes. The warm water then flows into a storage tank. There is only one disadvantage of solar panels. They work in bright sunlight but not on cloudy days! We have a lot to learn about collecting solar energy and converting it into heat and electrical power. Maybe people will drive solar-powered cars in the future.

The sun warms the atmosphere and gives plants energy to make food. It is the source of all life on Earth.

Can we catch sunlight?

In the *More Power!* experiment, we used a magnifying glass to collect sunlight and focus it onto a solar cell. Large **concave** mirrors that curve inward can also be used to reflect sunlight onto a small area. With so much sunlight concentrated in one place, the area receives a lot more solar energy than usual. Imagine a bottle standing in the rain. Very little rain can enter the bottle's narrow neck. A wide-mouthed funnel can catch more rain and channel the water into the bottle. Similarly, concave mirrors are able to catch more sunlight!

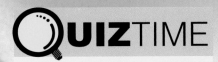

Did you know?

Scientists are studying ways to use solar furnaces to collect enough energy from the sun to generate power for homes, schools, offices, and factories. The world's largest solar furnace (*right*) is in Odeillo, France, in the Pyrenees Mountains. The Odeillo furnace has 9,600 moving mirrors spread over an area of 20,021 square feet (1,860 square m). The moving mirrors track the sun and focus the light onto other mirrors that form a large curved wall. This wall of mirrors reflects the sunlight onto a furnace. Temperatures in the furnace can reach 6332°F (3500°C).

EXPENSIVE ENERGY!

Solar energy is a clean source of energy—it does not pollute the Earth. But it is not a popular source of energy. The amount of solar energy that reaches the Earth in two weeks is equal to the world's production of energy from oil, coal, and gas in a year! Large collectors that catch and store solar energy are expensive. Until our regular fuels are used up, it costs too much to use solar energy on a large scale.

Why do sidewalks crack?

Cracks in sidewalks are often caused by heat expansion. Solids, liquids, and gases grow in size, or **expand**, when heated. When cooled, they decrease in size, or **contract**. What happens if there is no space for an object to expand or contract? Let's do a simple experiment to find out!

Difficult — 5
— 4
Moderate — 3
— 2
Easy — 1

You will need:
- A small bottle
- A small, deflated balloon
- An elastic band
- A bowl of hot water
- A bowl of cold water

Hot water balloon pump!

1 Remove the cap from the bottle. Wrap the deflated balloon over the mouth of the bottle. Seal it using the elastic band.

2 Place the bottle in the bowl of hot water. Watch what happens. After a while, the balloon inflates!

3 Now place the bottle in the bowl of cold water and watch what happens. The balloon starts to deflate!

Now, try another fun experiment.
Ask an adult for help.

Difficult – 5
– 4
Moderate – 3
– 2
Easy – 1

You will need:
- A small, narrow-necked bottle
- Cold and hot water
- Food coloring
- A piece of string, 12 inches (30 centimeters) long
- A large glass jar

Water genie!

1 Fill the bottle with cold water. Add drops of food coloring until the water is completely colored.

2 Tie the string securely around the neck of the bottle, leaving a long loose end.

3 Fill three-quarters of the jar with hot water. Then, holding the string, slowly lower the bottle into the jar. Keep the bottle upright.

4 Watch closely what happens as the bottle sinks into the hot water. Clouds of colored water burst from the bottle and spread over the surface of the hot water!

5 Keep watching the explosion of color. Eventually, the hot and cold water mixes completely and becomes one color.

Heat makes things bigger!

Objects expand when they are heated and contract when they cool. This happens because everything, from water to concrete, is made up of millions of tiny particles called molecules. The molecules of solid objects are arranged close together, the molecules of liquids are arranged farther apart, and the molecules of gases are arranged even farther apart. When something is heated, its molecules spread out.

In the *Hot Water Balloon Pump* experiment, the hot water in the bowl heated the air in the bottle, causing the balloon to inflate. When the bottle was placed in cold water, the air molecules in the bottle moved closer together, creating a **vacuum**, an empty space. Air from the balloon rushed into the bottle to fill the vacuum, causing the balloon to deflate. In the *Water Genie* experiment, the hot water in the jar heated the cold, colored water in the bottle. The water molecules in the bottle moved apart, and the water flowed out of the bottle.

Railway tracks are made of steel. In summer, the steel tracks expand and become longer. A special way of laying the tracks allows them to grow longer without bending.

Can we use heat expansion?

Heat expansion can be useful. For example, it enables steel tires to be fitted securely around the wheels of a train. A train tire is slightly smaller in **diameter** than a train wheel. The tire is heated with a ring of gas burners so that it expands. It becomes slightly larger than the wheel and can be slipped easily onto the wheel. When the tire cools, it contracts back to its original size. It presses tightly onto the wheel and cannot fall off easily. In thermometers, when the air around the bulb gets hot, the liquid in the bulb expands into the tube, and the thread rises.

A thermometer uses heat expansion to measure temperature.

Did you know?

Water does not always expand as it gets hotter. If we heat ice from 14°F (-10°C), it expands as its temperature rises to 32°F (0°C). At this temperature, melting ice (*right*) starts to contract! The water from the ice will expand again only when the temperature rises above 39.2°F (4°C).

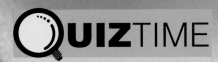

NO ROOM TO MOVE!

A concrete surface cracks when it has no space to expand. As the concrete increases in size, it runs out of space. It pushes upward and cracks. To prevent or reduce cracking in sidewalks, concrete is laid down in slabs with gaps in between the slabs. When the concrete expands, the slabs grow bigger and fill the gaps. Railway tracks also have gaps at intervals, so that separate sections of rail can lengthen freely on hot days.

How heat travels

Heat travels in three ways: conduction, radiation, and convection. **Conduction** carries heat through solids and liquids; **radiation** carries heat through gases; and **convection** carries heat through liquids and gases. Try this conduction experiment.

Difficult — 5
— 4
Moderate — 3
— 2
Easy — 1

You will need:
- A lighter or matches
- A candle
- A metal ruler
- A jar of boiling water

WATCH OUT!

Be careful when lighting the candle and dripping the wax on the ruler. Do not touch the ruler when it is hot. Ask an adult to help you.

1 With an adult's help, light the candle and carefully drip the wax onto one end of the metal ruler. Allow the wax to solidify, or harden.

Which melts first?

2 Place the unwaxed end of the ruler in the jar of boiling water. Watch which drop of wax melts first.

16

Do the wax melting experiment again, but use different materials this time. See how fast wax melts on iron and on wood!

Difficult — 5
— 4
Moderate — 3
— 2
Easy — 1

You will need:
- A lighter or matches
- A candle
- A wooden rod and an iron rod of the same size
- A jar of boiling water

Hot rods!

WATCH OUT!

Be careful when lighting the candle and dripping the wax on the rods. Do not touch the rods when they are hot. Ask an adult to help you.

1 With an adult's help, light the candle, and carefully drip the wax onto one end of each rod. Allow the wax to solidify, or harden.

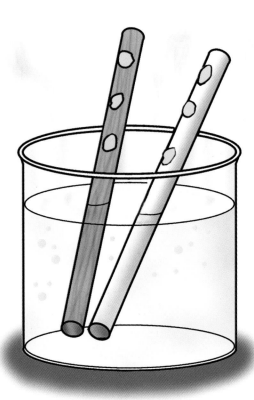

2 Place the unwaxed ends of both rods into the boiling water. Watch the wax on both rods. On which rod does the wax melt first?

17

How does heat travel?

Objects that are hot always lose heat to the colder things around them. This process is called thermal conduction. Materials such as rubber, wood, air, and water are poor **conductors**, because heat does not travel well through them. Objects made from metals such as iron are good conductors, because heat travels easily through them.

In the *Which Melts First?* experiment, heat from the boiling water moved along the ruler until it reached the wax drops on the upper end. The wax closest to the hot water melted first, because heat from the water reached that wax drop first.

Heat insulators are built into the roof, walls, and floor to protect the interior of this home from the winter cold.

What is Fourier's law?

Fourier's law states that how fast heat moves between two places depends on the temperature difference between the two places. The greater the difference in temperature, the faster heat travels. For example, heat will move quickly up a metal ruler if one end is covered in ice, and the other end is dipped in boiling water. The law was named after Jean-Baptise Joseph Fourier (*above*), the French mathematician who discovered it in 1822.

Winter clothing keeps us warm by trapping air. The layer of air acts like a heat shield. It slows down the release of heat away from the body.

Did you know?

Pots and pans are made from steel. Steel is a good conductor. It carries heat from the source to the food. The handles of pots and pans are often made from plastic or wood. Plastic and wood are poor conductors. They prevent the flow of heat to our hands, allowing us to hold the pots and pans.

ENERGY SAVER!

Poor conductors help us conserve energy in the home. Lining the walls with **insulation** keeps the house warmer in cold weather. In cold climates, the windows of homes and buildings are often double-glazed, meaning that they have two layers of glass with air in between. Air is a poor conductor, so it traps heat and keeps the cold out. Double-glazed windows cut down on energy needed to heat a building.

Why does it rain?

It rains when wet air cools and forms droplets that fall from the sky. Air picks up moisture from warm bodies of water by convection. Convection happens when heat is transferred by the circulation of air or water. The following experiments show how temperature changes can create convection currents.

You will need:
- A small circular plate
- A sheet of construction paper
- A pencil
- Scissors
- A piece of string, 6 inches (15 cm) long
- A toaster oven

A spinning spiral!

1 Place the plate face down on the construction paper. Using the pencil, trace a circle around the plate.

2 Carefully cut out the circle on the construction paper. Using the sharp point of the scissors, make a small hole in the middle of the circle.

3 Starting from the hole in the middle, draw a spiraling line outward to the edge. Then cut along the spiraling line from the edge to the middle.

4 Tie a knot at one end of the string, and thread the string through the center hole. Make sure the knot is bigger than the hole, so that the knot does not slip through.

5 Turn the toaster oven on. Ask an adult to help you hold the paper spiral over the warm toaster oven (never an open flame). Watch what happens. The paper spiral starts twirling!

20

Water volcano!

You will need:
- Two identical wide-necked glass bottles
- Cold and warm water
- Food coloring
- A stiff plastic sheet
- Plasticine

Difficult — 5
— 4
Moderate — 3
— 2
Easy — 1

1 Fill one bottle with cold water and the other with warm water. Add a few drops of food coloring to the bottle of warm water.

2 With one hand, hold the plastic sheet firmly over the mouth of the bottle containing the warm water. Slowly turn the bottle upside down, and place it over the bottle of cold water. Make sure the mouths of the two bottles meet exactly.

3 Hold the top bottle, and carefully slide the plastic sheet out from in between the two bottles. Watch for any movement of the colored water.

warm water

cold water

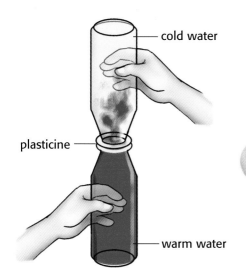

cold water

plasticine

warm water

4 Using the plasticine, seal the two bottle mouths together to make them watertight. Reverse the bottles so that the cold water is on top and the warm water is at the bottom. Now watch the movement of the colored water!

Circles of air and water!

Why did the paper spiral twirl over the hot toaster oven? The answer is convection. Convection happens when heat is transferred in a gas or liquid by the circulation of currents. Hot air rises and travels and is replaced by cooler air in a circular motion. This circulation is called a convection current. When the air around the toaster oven warmed up, it expanded. The lighter warm air rose, and the heavier cool air sank.

The same thing happened in the *Water Volcano* experiment. When the bottle of warm water was on top, the colored water did not flow into the bottle of cold water. This is because the warm water was lighter than the cold water. When the bottles were reversed, the lighter warm water rose, and the heavier cold water sank. This created a water current, which was shown by the movement of the food coloring.

Warm water has a different **density** than cold water. This causes warm ocean water (red) and cold ocean water (blue) to move around the world. The movement of ocean water disperses heat around the Earth. It also churns up nutrients from the sea floor to feed marine life.

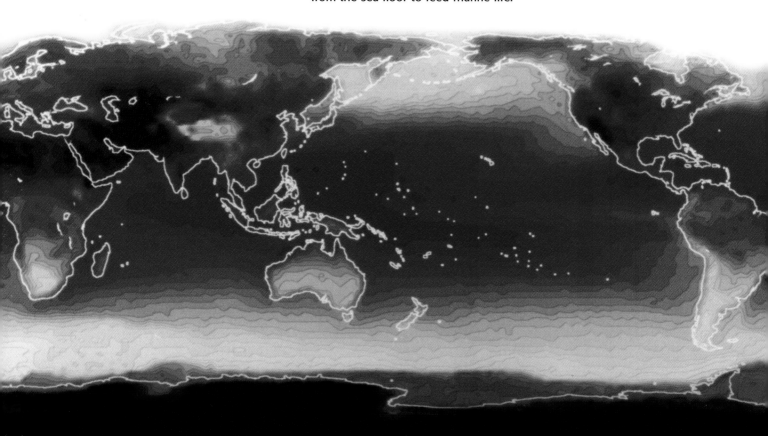

Convection in the sky...

Convection in the Earth's atmosphere creates air currents that affect the weather. When a large body of warm air rises, cool air moves in to take its place. This creates a breeze. When warm air rises, it cools and condenses. This forms clouds of water droplets, which fall as rain.

... and in the sea

Ocean waters are constantly moving. The sun heats the waters in the tropics. The warm water flows toward the poles. It displaces cold water from the poles. The cold water flows toward the equator. This cycle never ends. The cold water flowing to the equator warms up and flows back to the poles. Warm water flowing to the poles cools down and flows back to the equator.

Water boils in a kettle through the circulation of hot and cold water.

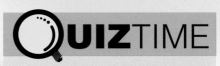

Liquid rock beneath the Earth's crust rises and is released through volcanoes.

Did you know?

Convection takes place even on the sun! The sun transfers heat from its interior to its surface by convection. The core of the sun, the hottest part, sends columns of hot gases rising to the surface. At the surface, the gases release their heat into space and then sink to the core to be reheated.

CONVECTION DEEP UNDERGROUND!

Convection also occurs in the molten rock beneath the Earth's crust. Molten rock closest to the Earth's core is the hottest and lightest. It rises toward the crust. Molten rock closest to the crust is cooler. It is heavier and sinks. This exchange of material between crust and core creates convection currents, which move huge pieces of the Earth's crust known as tectonic plates. The tectonic plates move closer together or farther apart, forming mountains and trenches.

23

A heat wave!

Heat energy moves through gases in the form of waves. Heat waves travel by radiation and are absorbed differently by different objects to varying degrees. Try this experiment to find out which surfaces absorb more heat energy than others!

Difficult — 5
— 4
Moderate — 3
— 2
Easy — 1

Hot and hotter!

1 Tear two pieces of aluminum foil so that both pieces are equal in size. Paint one side of one piece of foil with black paint.

WATCH OUT!
Ask an adult to help you with this experiment. Light bulbs can get very hot.

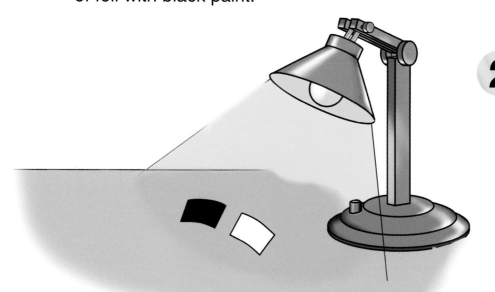

2 After the paint is dry, place both pieces of foil directly under the lamp. Turn the lamp on.

3 Turn the lamp off after about one minute. Carefully touch each of the pieces of foil. Which one is hotter?

Now, we know how the sun's heat reaches us. It travels through space by radiation. This experiment will show you how hot the sun's rays can be!

Difficult — 5
— 4
Moderate — 3
— 2
Easy — 1

You will need:
- A glass bottle
- An open window
- A piece of white paper
- A thermometer

Red hot!

1 On a sunny day, place the glass bottle near the window so that sunlight passes through it.

2 Hold up the piece of white paper behind the bottle so that sunlight shines through the bottle and onto the paper. Adjust the distance between the paper and the bottle, until a spectrum of seven colors appears on the paper.

3 Place the bulb of the thermometer near the red side of the rainbow. Watch the temperature rise!

4 Note the temperature of the red strip. Now, take the temperature of the other colors. Which is the hottest color of the rainbow?

Heat knows no bounds!

In conduction and convection, objects have to touch one another in order for heat to move. Radiation can transmit heat without direct contact between objects. In fact, heat can travel through a vacuum by radiation!

In the *Red Hot* experiment, why did the red strip of the rainbow have a higher temperature than the other colors? This is because **infrared** radiation, or heat from the sun, is concentrated in the red strip. Infrared radiation comes from the sun and travels through space to warm up the planets in the solar system.

Heat from the sun travels through the vacuum of space to the planets in the solar system by the process of radiation.

To absorb or not to absorb...

In the *Hot and Hotter* experiment, why did the black piece of foil feel warmer than the silver one? It felt warmer because dark and dull surfaces are good absorbers of heat. They absorb more heat than bright and shiny surfaces. Good absorbers are also good emitters. They release heat. Dark and dull surfaces are good absorbers and good emitters of heat. In contrast, bright and shiny surfaces are poor absorbers and poor emitters of heat.

These houses in a town in Greece stay cool with white walls that reflect heat.

Stay cool!

We can use our knowledge of radiation to our advantage. Buildings painted in white or light colors stay cooler in summer, because their bright walls reflect the sun's heat. Similarly, light-colored clothing keeps us cooler in hot weather, and dark clothing keeps us warmer in colder weather.

A street vendor sits comfortably under the shade of a white umbrella.

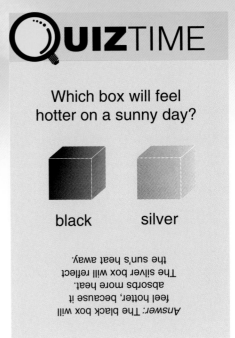

QUIZTIME

Which box will feel hotter on a sunny day?

black   silver

Answer: The black box will feel hotter, because it absorbs more heat. The silver box will reflect the sun's heat away.

 Did you know?

A thermos has two glass walls separated by a vacuum. This protects the contents of the thermos from heat loss by conduction and convection. The inner surface of each of the two walls is coated with a thin layer of silver. Since shiny surfaces are poor emitters, they slow down the passage of heat across the vacuum between the walls.

 GLOBAL GREENHOUSE!

The Earth's atmosphere acts like a greenhouse. Most of the sun's heat that enters the Earth's atmosphere is absorbed by the Earth's surface. Some heat is reflected back into the atmosphere. **Greenhouse gases**, such as carbon dioxide, trap the reflected radiation in the atmosphere, creating a greenhouse effect. Normally, greenhouse gases are not harmful. By trapping heat, they keep the planet warm. Human activities, such as burning fossil fuels, add to the natural greenhouse gases in the atmosphere. This overheats the Earth and creates environmental problems, such as melting polar icecaps and rising sea levels.

27

What is heat capacity?

Heat capacity is the amount of heat an object needs to get warm. Does the size of an object affect how quickly it heats up? Find out with this experiment!

You will need:
- Water
- A measuring cup
- A small pot
- A thermometer
- A stove
- A stopwatch
- Pen and paper

More or less?

1 Fill 3/4 of the measuring cup (200 ml) with water. Transfer the water to a small pot. Ask an adult to turn on the stove on high, and place the pot on the stove burner.

2 Put the bulb of the thermometer in the water. Start heating the water. At the same time, start the stopwatch. When the thermometer shows that the temperature of the water has reached 140°F (60°C), write down the time shown on the stopwatch.

3 Ask an adult to help you empty the pot. (You can use the hot water to make hot chocolate.)

4 Now, measure 1 1/2 cups (400 ml) of water using the measuring cup. Transfer the water to the small pot. Place the pot on the burner on high, and put the bulb of the thermometer in the water. Start heating the water and start the stopwatch. Note the time it takes for the temperature of the water to reach 140°F.

5 Compare the two records. Which **volume** of water reached 140°F faster? Why?

28

Does the type of material an object is made from affect how quickly it heats up? Try this quick and easy activity to see how two different liquids react to the same amount of heat.

Two temperatures on one hand!

Difficult — 5
— 4
Moderate — 3
— 2
Easy — 1

You will need:
- A dropper
- Rubbing alcohol
- Water

1 Using the dropper, put a drop of rubbing alcohol and a drop of water onto the back of your hand.

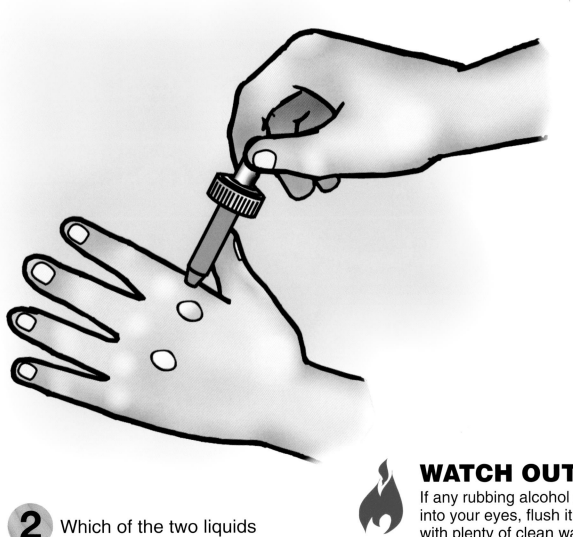

2 Which of the two liquids feels cooler? Why?

WATCH OUT!
If any rubbing alcohol gets into your eyes, flush it out with plenty of clean water.

Enter a world of heat capacities!

Why did 1 1/2 cups (400 ml) of water take a longer time than 3/4 of a cup (200 ml) of water to reach 140°F (60°C)? Why did a drop of rubbing alcohol feel cooler on your hand than a drop of water? The answer to both questions is heat capacity. Heat capacity is the amount of heat needed to raise the temperature of an object by one degree. Two factors affect heat capacity: substance (what it is made of) and size (how big it is).

Alcohol evaporates faster than water, because it has a lower heat capacity. It needs less heat to rise in temperature. Since it evaporates faster, alcohol removes heat from a surface faster and therefore feels cooler on the skin. A larger volume of water has a higher heat capacity than a smaller volume of water. This is why it took longer to heat 1 1/2 cups (400 ml) than 3/4 of a cup (200 ml) of water to the same temperature.

Lying on the beach feels warmer than splashing in the water. This is because the heat capacity of water is higher than that of sand.

What is specific heat?

Specific heat refers to the amount of heat needed to raise the temperature of one gram (0.035 ounces) of a substance by 1°C, or 1.8°F. One gram of iron, for example, needs slightly more heat energy than one gram of gold to rise in temperature by 1°C. In 1819, two French chemists made an interesting discovery. Pierre Louis Dulong (*left*) and Alexis Thérèse Petit found a formula using specific heat to calculate how heavy one atom of any substance weighs.

Did you know?

The unit for measuring heat energy is called the joule. The joule was named after the British scientist James Joule, who proved in the mid-1800s that heat was a form of energy. The unit for measuring food energy is called the calorie. Humans need to consume calories in order to live. We use or "burn" calories as "fuel" through daily living. Some foods, such as fast food (*right*), contain many calories.

LAND AND SEA BREEZES

Water has a higher heat capacity than rock or soil. This means that the sea takes a longer time than the land to warm up under the sun. When hot air over the land rises, cool air moves in from the sea to take its place. This results in sea breezes, which keep coastal areas cool in summer. A higher heat capacity also means that water takes longer than land to cool down at night. Warm air over the sea rises, and cool air moves in from the land to take its place, creating a land breeze.

Glossary

atoms (page 3): Tiny particles found in every object.

concave (page 11): Curved or hollowed inward like the inside of a circle.

conduction (page 16): The transfer of heat from a warm to a cool place.

conductors (page 18): Materials that readily carry heat energy from a hot object to a cooler one.

contract (page 12): To decrease in size.

convection (page 16): The distribution of heat in a circulating gas or liquid.

current (page 9): The flow of electricity.

density (page 22): The amount of mass in a substance.

diameter (page 15): A straight line dividing a circle into equal halves.

diesel (page 6): A fuel used in car engines. It is heavier and oilier than gasoline.

electricity (page 4): Energy that powers objects such as cars and lamps.

expand (page 12): To increase in size.

galvanometer (page 9): A device for detecting small electrical currents.

greenhouse gases (page 27): Gases that trap heat in the Earth's atmosphere.

infrared (page 26): The red end of the light spectrum, where most of the sun's heat is concentrated.

insulation (page 19): Material that does not easily carry heat energy from a hot object to a cooler one.

matter (page 3): Anything that takes up space, whether solid, liquid, or gas.

molecules (page 3): The smallest particles of matter, consisting of one or more atoms.

pistons (page 6): Devices consisting of an inner cylinder moving within an outer cylinder, due to liquid or gas pressure.

radiation (page 16): The process by which heat spreads out in the form of waves.

solar cell (page 9): A device which converts light energy to electrical energy.

turbines (page 7): Devices consisting of rotating blades attached to a shaft, used to power electrical generators.

vacuum (page 14): An empty space completely without matter.

volume (page 28): The amount of space a substance occupies.

vapor (page 6): Liquid that has turned to gas.

Index